Treasures o

Treasures of Darkness

Clare Gregg

Heavensent Publications

Treasures of Darkness

Published by Heavensent Publications
Copyright © Clare Gregg 2006

Heavensent Publications.
P. O. Box 327,
Gateshead,
NE8 4ZX
www.heavensentpublications.com
e-mail: info@heavensentpublications.com

Clare Gregg is hereby identified as the Author
in accordance with copyright 2006.

Unless stated all Bible quotations are taken from the NIV-New
International Version. Copyright with permission.
Moravian hymn book.

ISBN
1-905661-00-2
978-1-905661-00-8

Printed and bound in Great Britain by
Martins the Printers Limited, Sea View Works, Spittal, Berwick-upon-Tweed
www.martins-the-printers.com

Treasures of Darkness

Foreword

CHRIST says, *"I have come as a light into the world, that whoever believes in me should not remain in darkness" (John 12:46).*

Some years ago I heard a curate say, *"Use your pit for a well"*. I cannot remember what misery prompted this remark but the thought was so descriptive that it has never left me.

It seems to me that this book is an example of doing just that, allowing God by His love, to transform the very pain and suffering we encounter, for whatever reason, to become lasting treasure for His glory.

Each life is a unique journey, but there is powerful testimony in overcoming satan's wiles through our Lord Jesus Christ. The author has illuminated her thoughts with living words of scripture. When drawn to verse 3 in Isaiah 45, *"I will give you the treasures of darkness, riches stored in secret places, so that you may know that I am the Lord, the God of Israel, who summons you by name."*…. These words are part of God's prophesy about what He would do through Cyrus, King of Persia, 100 years before his time!

In 538 BC, the first year of his reign over Babylon, when through the mouth of Jeremiah the prophesy in Isaiah, concerning him, was told to Cyrus, his spirit was stirred up by God, so that His purpose to release His people Israel, after 70 years of captivity and bondage in Babylon would be accomplished. In the book of Ezra Chapter one it is recorded how Cyrus responded to God's word, that he should build Him a house at Jerusalem. Thus the willing Jews were freed, with material assistance, from their neighbours to go up to Jerusalem under Zerubbabel to rebuild the temple and city.

Cyrus was God's instrument for liberation. Isaiah's wonderful prophesy names Cyrus and calls him anointed for this special purpose. The *"treasures of darkness"* promised to Cyrus referred to Egyptian booty and the control of Egyptian trade routes.

Here is a shadow of the liberation to come in God's plan and purpose through His Son Jesus Christ, in the New Testament. Victory over the prince of darkness and his bondage of sin, sickness and death; satan's trade marks and routes, was won through the darkness of Christ's cross where Jesus broke forever the power of our enemy and brought for us new life in Him, the light of life. What a transformation!

Life is a test and a trust. A test because we are fallen and imperfect and a trust that indeed God will *"make all things new" (Revelations 21:5).*

Being born again out of darkness into light, out of hatred into love, out of depression into joy, out of fear into faith, out of death into life is a first step. There is so much more with Jesus who does the impossible, the liberator and saviour of us all.

> *"Jesus Sun of righteousness,*
> *Brightest beams of love divine*
> *With early morning rays,*
> *Do thou on our darkness shine,*
> *And dispel with purest light*
> *All our night."*
>
> Jane Borthwick

Let the reader be blessed.

Helen Weir.

Treasures of Darkness

Preface

WHY have I chosen, having written a book on walking in the light, to write on darkness, the trial of darkness, not the deeds of darkness. Sin can lead to a Godly trial, as we choose again an upward path of righteousness. We are to be wise about the world's ways. The world is in the grip of darkness. People are sometimes forced to be in darkness in prison, at work and in relationship. Too much light at the wrong time damages. It damages spiritually, as with light touching a photographic film. In the physical world it can blind, burn, causing the total destruction of a fire. The fiercest sunlight kills.

Too much exposure of our person harms us emotionally and spiritually. The truth will appear a lie if we do not know or understand ourselves. Forced exposure damages, as in an investigative situation we are forced to speak. Wrong exposure wrecks and ruins, we are unable to face reality in the presence of our enemies. It is to be the work of God's Holy Spirit. God's grace is much more forebearing. *"Love covers a multitude of sins." (1 Peter 4:8).* For God to expose and to bring into the light a specific sin or sinful pattern of behaviour takes time. He is not willing that a reputation is ruined; His desire is to forgive and heal. There can be a night of judgement. He expects us to repent. The light is a blessing as others forgive. There are places in scripture where God gives refuge to someone who has sinned and hides them. He hides them in the darkness and privacy of the night. God can love, heal and forgive us. There are no intrusive and prying eyes. *(Psalm 31:20)*. It is God's presence that sustains us.

I have also written on darkness, because of the negative association of light with satan falling like lightening *(Luke 10:18)* and being referred to as an angel of light. And because people blatantly do evil in broad day light, and although these deeds are done in the light are deeds of darkness. *(2 Peter 2:13-15)*. Evil known about is to be repented of, if unrepented of harms and hurts.

Introduction

DARKNESS holds fear for many. The darkness of the physical night, with the associations of evil, and the fear of the unknown. It is easier to get lost physically and emotionally. The fear of the spiritual night because of our inability to find God's presence, or to understand His dealings and His guiding hand. Both evil and spiritual darkness can be conquered, as well as our fear of the night. For other darkness is a comfort because of its privacy. It is a secret place, a place of hiding.

We need to separate the deeds of darkness that are evil from the protection of the night, as God hides us from wicked men. Darkness is as light to the Lord. The world is in the grips of darkness, as are people outside Christ.

Darkness itself is not to hold fear for people in Christ. It is created by God and known to Him. Nothing is hidden from Him. And the evil of darkness is defeated on the cross of Calvary. God anoints his people to discern truth from error. His presence and protection are with us in darkness. He is *"light shining in a dark place, until the day dawns and the morning star arises in your hearts." (2 Peter 1:19).*

Even the most obedient to the gospel of Christ can find themselves in a dark night of trial, through no fault of our own. It can be a time of growth as our spiritual understanding increases. Darkness is caused by others sin and deception, and our inability to understand our compromise, caused by fear or rebellion. It is God's word the entrance, and understanding of that word that gives light. There is now no condemnation in Christ Jesus. He can lead us victoriously through to the light having in that darkness shared with us hidden treasures, secrets of wisdom of His will, way, and His heart. The trial of the night ends, as will pain and suffering.

Chapter 1

The place of darkness in creation

"I am the Lord, and there is no other. I form the light and create darkness." (Isaiah 45:7).

GOD chose to form from what was formless, empty and dark, the whole of creation. God created day and night. He chose there to be light in the darkness, the moon and the stars and He called that night. Without the moon and the stars the night is total darkness. *(Genesis 1:16-18)*. God separated darkness from light, calling the light day but He still chose for there to be times and places of darkness in creation. We must not fear the blackest night. God created black and white. *"I will give you the treasures of darkness, riches stored in secret places, so that you may know that I am the Lord."* In *(Isaiah 45:3)*; Secret place implies hidden places; private places, and intimate places. God will teach us in the darkest night spiritually, that as the night and the darkness pass and the day and the light come, so in our lives the light appears as we understand spiritually God's dealings. Night turns to day. Our darkness to light. Darkness is as light to the Lord from Him nothing is hidden.

Sometimes people have to work in physical darkness, and at night. That night also ends.

What is formed in darkness

Beautiful, real, good and living things as well as precious stones, so in our lives He can make something precious out of what is dark, formless and empty.

a) Real treasures, with all their value and worth and implications of eternity, are formed and mined from the deepest darkness of the earth's furnace. Gold, emeralds, diamonds and rubies. That beauty is reflected in us as we are changed from one degree of glory to another. It is those treasures given to us in the darkness and pressure of the refiner's fire that give point and purpose to our darkest night.

b) Living plants with all their beauty and their uses. The oak formed, so the birds of the air can be sheltered is formed in complete darkness from a tiny seed, under ground, under pressure to show itself as a huge tree needing and depending entirely on the light. There is spiritual parallel, God can make us those *"oaks of righteousness"* to protect care and shelter others although made from a tiny beginning.

c) Babies are formed in pitch black, complete darkness. It is that dark place that is seen to be a place of protection, for the growing foetus. Babies are not scanned at a late date for fear of harming them with the light of an intrusive eye. A possible enemies 'eye' with intent to harm and disrupt. But as plants, babies grow in the darkness to live and walk in the light.

d) Us, often the person we are, our characters and personalities are formed secretly in relationship with God. This is because another's criticism harms us. God shares with us His secrets, of His will and way, often in the darkest night spiritually and sometimes physically. We are to learn to change our darkest wounding, our pain and our sin by God's grace into treasures, accepting the truth of God's presence and word.

God forms us often in dark places spiritually and physically. There is no merit in the darkness, nor the negative emotions that cause that darkness. But the fact that God works in the darkness, and His presence can be found is truth. He works in the darkness because darkness is as light to Him. It is often in those places of trial and darkness, that God shares with us the secrets of His will and way making us like Him. He gives us and makes us treasures. He gives treasures of faith character, obedience, perseverance and wisdom, planting positive as opposed to negative truths in our inner most being. But we do not easily feel that presence or know that light. But we have to choose to rely upon our God, and not to choose to do the evil deeds of darkness. Because we can despair that God appears to bless the wicked in our night of darkness. It is as we learn to walk by faith we become more Christ-like, treasured by him.

Chapter 2

Victory over darkness

<u>Fear of darkness and overcoming that fear</u>

WE can fear darkness because of the unknown. The association of evil, or an evil presence. This can be spiritual darkness. It can also be the real fear of physical darkness, the night, or an enclosed place without light.

We need to know:

i) God's presence as a fact. That the presence of God's Holy Spirit is more powerful than any demonic force or evil. In a dark time of apprehension, with fear of loss, of God's presence, power, and protection we are to understand God is with us. His promise is not to leave, or to forsake us. We are to use the shield of faith.

ii) Understand God's protection is real. He is an ever present help in times of trouble.

iii) Know God is working for our good, in a trial

5

of darkness. He will teach us His will, and way, and bring us through to a more fruitful place.

iv) Know it is the entrance of God's word that gives light, to let the word of Christ dwell in us richly. Perfect love casts out fear. God is love, and Jesus is the word made flesh. God's words are loving and faithful.

v) Understand that darkness is as light to the Lord, so what is darkness to us is still light to Him. *"Surely the darkness will hide me and the light become night around me, even the darkness will not be dark to you, the night will shine like the day for darkness is as light to you." (Psalm 139: 11-12).* He knows the way. We are to trust in the Lord's hand of guidance who has complete knowledge and understanding.

vi) Understanding that in God's will, and plan, there is a point and purpose to our times of darkness. He is able to refine us in the refiner's fire, so we will be changed into His likeness, from one degree of glory to another. It is in the darkness, that he shares His secrets with us and gives His treasures. Treasures of faith, not fear. *"I will give you treasures of darkness, riches stored in secret places, so that you may know that I am the Lord, the God of Israel that summons you by name." (Isaiah 45:3).* Everyone likes secrets, gifts hidden. There are also the dark secrets, that is not what God is referring to; but even the darkest secret or sin known to another, brings light and forgiveness. It is then for us to repent.

Spiritual darkness

This can be caused by:

1. Sin: All sin is darkness in a spiritual sense. Until our sin is confessed, and repented of there is darkness. The blood of Jesus has to cleanse and purify us, for us to be in a place of forgiveness. Outside the torture of condemnation, and the blackness of associated emotions.

2. Loss: The experience of spiritual darkness caused by loss. There are dark nights of divorce, or the death of a loved one, that bring loneliness and separation. They may feel betrayed by the deceased person, as if death were their choice, to reject them leaving them alone. They blame not God but the deceased for their night. There are the dark nights of financial and spiritual loss.

3. Failure, repeated failure: A failed deep

relationship or 'string of relationships' causes darkness. An inability, or failure to understand the gospel of Christ, or a failed career.

4. Mistrust: The experience of the mental distress when we do not trust another person. We are in a state of suspicion, as opposed to confidence and trust in another person's fidelity and motive for our good. Suspicion and mistrust are dark emotions. We are always to attempt to find out about the truth. The reality of an event or person, because suspicion is either real, or unfounded. And that person either, can or cannot, be trusted. If they can be trusted then we are to be healed, and forgiven of our mistrust. If not and our suspicion founded then we are to trust in the Lord with all our heart. It will be our confidence in His unfailing love, His dependability and trustworthiness that enable us to cope. It becomes our ability to walk on water with our God, with maturity and wisdom that sustains us. The Lord is our confidence. And from that secure place, we can still be in relationship with another not as trustworthy. Knowledge of the truth, of another's behaviour keeps reality in our lives. We can also keep in reality by letting the truth of God's word dwell in us richly. We are to hide

God's word in our hearts.

5. Deception: causes darkness because it is not the truth but a lie. Satan is the *"father of lies"*. And lies cause darkness, because of the element of untruth, and the not knowing.

6. Unknown: Darkness is also due to the unknown. The unknown by its nature causes darkness and is in a sense darkness.

   We need 'light to be shed' on a situation. When we are sick and do not know what is wrong, we are in the dark, about the situation, and that illness. We choose a physician to shed light. They have knowledge that we do not have; as do the saints who have gone ahead of us. The Lord also gives words of insight, knowledge, and wisdom.

   It is the fact that the Lord, who is light and there is no darkness in Him, has His presence, protection and power in the dark that is the key to the treasures of darkness. His presence and protection, are in the dark. He has the ability to teach us by His word and to refine us by His Spirit.

7. Betrayal: The experience of betrayal can lead to the darkest night. A false witness, leading to a prison sentence and in Jesus's case to death on a cross. It was the officialdom of priests that

plotted against Jesus. He was finally betrayed. Then falsely accused and crucified. *(Matthew 26:2)*. We need to understand people cannot harm us outside God's will. It is with consent and foreknowledge, as on the cross.

8. Hardness of heart: *"They are darkened in their understanding and separated from the life of God because of the ignorance that is within them due to the hardening of their hearts." (Ephesians 4:18).* This was said of the gentiles outside Christ, but this darkened understanding can happen to us, as we harden our hearts in unbelief.

How do we get through our darkest night and what are the treasures God gives us, as our emotional and spiritual darkness is conquered

We get through our darkest night by:

a) Using God's word.
b) Other's experience and wisdom. They have conquered in their darkest night.
c) Our prior knowledge of God, and faith in His goodness.
d) By our perseverance. We are to persevere.
e) Conquering fear, with faith.

Victory over the darkness of fear

Fear is sin. There is the darkness of fear instead of faith. There are many fears. Fear of the dark, instead of faith in God's presence and protection. Fear of light, and being known. Fear of the unknown. Fear of places. Fear of people with an expectation of harm, without understanding they cannot harm without God's plan, purpose, foreknowledge and all things working together for our good. Fear of certain situations. Fear of success. God's will is for us to be successful and to prosper, some people lack this understanding. Fear of failure. Fear of rejection or an inability to accept others acceptance. We can even fear life itself. Jesus is the way the truth and the life.

The darkness of fear, and the negative destructive effect of that fear, can be healed. We need the light of Christ to identify and to understand our fear and the disability that it causes. *"With God all things are possible"* and understand prayer. *"Whatever two or three of you agree on earth it shall be done for you."* We are to PRAY:

"Dear Lord Jesus, from whom nothing is hidden, and who has all wisdom and knowledge we ask you reveal and heal our fears. We ask in Jesus name that .... (Name a person) fear of ....(name the fear e.g. success) is healed and replaced by an ability to accept......(e.g. success) and to understand success is

from God. His blessing."

We are to conquer the experience of fear replacing that with faith. This is only possible as we accept the truth of God's word. As we learn to conquer in the trial of fear; treasures of faith, wisdom and understanding are formed. Sometimes we have to overcome an enemy to defeat our fear. We need to discern who or what is attempting to hurt us and or our belongings. Enemies are to be overcome. Our fears can be founded, or they can be unfounded, and irrational and overcome by the truth of God's word. They can have their origins in the past formed by negative events and circumstances similar to the ones we are facing. They are to also be healed by prayer. Fears can be passed on and learnt from our parents. We have a fearful nature.

There is the fear of evil, and the feelings of the presence of evil. These can be overcome as we understand our place in Christ in the heavenlies. The ways in which God helps us, and teaches us, to defeat our fears are treasures. Fear can cause suffering. We are able to share in another's suffering, to fulfil the law of Christ and enable them to live without fear. As we use God's word treasures of faith are formed. We choose to learn to overcome our fears. We need an understanding of God's will in His word. As one of the deepest spiritual fears causing darkness is a fear we are outside Christ, outside a place of salvation. Outside His saving grace not in His will for our lives. A fear of not being forgiven, and eternally condemned, when fear is a feeling not a fact of reality. These fears can be banished by the truth of God's word. The blood of Jesus cleanses us from all unrighteousness. There is now no condemnation in Christ Jesus. We have the seal of God's Holy Spirit, as a seal of ownership and the good that is to come. *(2 Corinthians 1:21-22).*

We are to express our fear of being in the wrong or outside God's will. If we have known fear we are to learn faith in God's word of promise, and protection, to build our lives on rock, the truth and reality of God's word. We are to overcome.

Fear is also caused by the reality of evil in a presence or a person. We need to know God's protection, God's word the reality and truth of that word. We are to rely on others.

"Do not gloat over me, my enemy! Though I have fallen, I will rise. Though I sit in darkness the Lord will be my light, because I have sinned against Him I will bear the Lords' wrath" (Micah 7:8). When we have times of darkness it is important that we accept God's word is the truth, including the Old testament. *(2 Peter 1:19-21).* It is a light and lamp to our feet until the light of Christ shines for us, victorious again. Fear is a dark emotion. And all sin is darkness, fear, hatred, anger are

13

all to be overcome, to do so we need to have an understanding of why. Why we are fearful, what we fear and why our response is not faith. Why we hate, what we hate, why we choose not to love. It is often because of the element of the impossibility, the unknown we do not understand God's will and way completely. The task is too large and frightening. The unknown is a fearful state. We need to rely upon our God. There is a fear of falling, fear of failing, fear of darkness, fear of light, fear of being known, fear of success, fear of failure, fear of loss, fear of money, fear of poverty. We need to ask God that He shines His light into our hearts, minds, and emotions so we can understand and banish our fears.

Darkness as a destructive force is to be understood and overcome

Satan's plan is one of darkness in a destructive sense. For us never to see the light at the end of the tunnel. People are with out hope outside Christ, and in that place. Satan's plan is for us not to be forgiven, to remain outside Christ in death in a spiritual sense. Outside eternal salvation, and in sickness. All the images of darkness, as an evil belong to satan. Satan's plan is one of loss, of desolation of fear and hate. Where dread is the only expectancy. The evil of witchcraft, and all in opposition to God's plan and purpose, with their intent to hurt and harm are of satan. We have a fight of faith bringing the reality and truth of God's word into being. We are to speak the truth. *"The righteous will live by faith." (Romans1:17).* It is God's word, power, grace and the blood of Jesus that overcome every image and reality of evil, and darkness as a dark force caused by deeds of evil. This will bring us through to a place of fruitfulness. Jesus triumphed over evil as he experienced the darkest night of the cross, and made it possible for us to be victors over evil, bringing our lives through to a place of victorious living in the light. Jesus's night of desertion gave us life, and the ability to be in fellowship with one another. This is because the blood of Jesus removes the dividing wall of hostility. We are also to be aware that it was satan who fell like lightening, having tried to make himself above His creator God. It is God's plan to heal, satan's to make sick. God's plan to forgive, satan's to torture and condemn. Satan's plan for us to hate and be hated, God's plan for us to love and be loved. Jesus came to bring life, the devil to take. The devil's plan can bring a night, we are to learn to live victoriously using the sword of the Spirit, the word of God, in that night. God's plan is that we traverse that night, learning of Him.

We have the darkness of:

Trials

We are to understand to bring our lives through to a place of victory in Christ. It is in the darkest times that we can become the most bitter and twisted. This can happen to us in our Christian walk, by our choice because we have been repeatedly harmed and sinned against. We need to ask for God's protection from other people's hardness. Sometimes we feel the bitterness and hardness of another's sin. It is also the time when we can learn to be the most victorious. God will not give us more than we are able to forgive. His grace is able to enable us to forgive. For it is God's plan and purpose that prevails, and all things do work together for our good. This promise is for us, and for the person who chooses to ruin their life, by a wilful choice to harm us, as they repent and turn to Christ. We are to claim and understand God's ability and desire to be victorious in their lives. It is one of the most difficult things to happen, a restored relationship, rather than just a forgiven person.

We do not want to be in relationship with the person who has hurt us. We can forgive but restoration seems impossible. We are to attempt to learn new behaviour to be in relationship.

The darkness of the cross

One of the darkest moments, spiritually, physically and emotionally was on the cross for our Lord Jesus. He had real separation from His Heavenly Father, because of man's sin and the judgement of that sin, and sickness put on Him. Jesus who became like man in every way who was supposed to save us, the messiah, the anointed one seemingly a defeated man, the light of life finished in and by the darkness. The light of the world suffered total darkness, and separation from God. But He triumphed and up from the grave He rose. He triumphed over sickness, satan and his plan of total destruction. We can also triumph over a dark night of trial not chosen or welcomed by us.

Jesus at the end of His night, a short one, was given the highest place, and the name above all names. And having gone through that night was restored to His glory, with the ability for God's Holy Spirit to be poured out on us. So we can do greater works than Jesus did on earth. We too can increase our fruitfulness in our trial of the cross. The purpose of His dark night was to reconcile God to man. This was accomplished. Jesus would not have understood His night of impeding darkness, nor why sin and sickness had to be put on Him as an atoning sacrifice but it was through no fault of his own. He knew the cross was to happen, that it was God's will, set plan, and purpose. In a sense it was out of Jesus's control, including the victory of that night. But it was with Jesus's consent *"Yet not my will but yours be done." (Luke 22:42).* We have to trust God to carry us through our night of darkness in the same way; through to a place of victory and fruitfulness and into God's dream for our lives. Jesus did not *'get himself through'* the crucifixion to the resurrection God did, His mighty power at work within him. It was through no fault of His own, that Jesus was put on that cross, but like Jesus we will go through our cross, our night of trial to know God's resurrection power. Those places of darkness are often the making of God's plan for our lives. We were all created for a plan and a purpose. He who began the good work, will bring it to completion. The devil's plan and purpose did not prevail, God's did. We will also have prayed prayers choosing to be obedient to God's will and way, committing our way to Him. Sometimes it takes a night of trial to fulfil God's highest and best.

Whether like Jesus we have the darkest night of the cross put on our lives; or because of our choices and decisions, or because we accept another's deception and enter a night. We will have to, at some point, repent of our choice to be disobedient to God's word, having knowingly sinned. On repentance we will enter a cross-like trial as we are again guided by God's word. And like all others with a burden too heavy, the love of Christ will carry us. There is an element of passivity and a degree of dependency, as we go through a night, our time of darkness. Just as it was God who gave His people unity. *(2 Chronicles 30:12).*

People sometimes cannot put into words the terror of their night. Their separation from God real or emotional, or from a loved one. About an imprisonment, or the betrayal of being wrongly accused, possibly having been tried and convicted as an innocent person and the night this causes. There is the dark night spiritually until the truth sets us free and the unknown is known. An infidelity and betrayal of a husband or wife which goes unexpressed for fear of: a) Being mis-understood; fault and blame wrongly placed. b) Fear of loosing your spouse. c) Fear of failure being seen by another. d) Fear of disrespect. e) Or because the choice is to continue to betray. f)But it is often our unbelief and frozen numbness that prevents us expressing our fear about the truth we are rendered speechless. It causes terrible darkness and continued suspicion.

We can choose to sin and make for ourselves a man-made cross. We also have to see in that the hand of God. Our lives were not refined enough, not built enough on rock the truth of God's word. God can refine us, heal us and establish His Lordship in our lives. God is a *"guide for the blind, a light for those who are in darkness." (Romans 2:19)*. He is with us lighting the way, *"a light shining in a dark place, until the day dawns and the morning star rises in your hearts." (2 Peter 1:19)* until we are set free by the truth.

The darkness of the cross caused by sin and disobedience

Darkness can be to do with God not relenting from calamity. It is to do with God's judgement because of our sin and often resulting sickness. When Jesus was crucified there was real darkness that came over the earth, as our judgement was put on Him. So that we could be forgiven and accept the light of Christ. *"From the sixth hour to the ninth hour darkness came over all the land."* (Matthew 27:45-46).

Everything to do with the cross was darkness. Darkness was let to reign. Jesus said: *"Everyday I was with you in the temple courts, and you did not lay a hand on me. But this is your hour – when darkness reigns." (Luke 22:53).* If Jesus understood it was the enemies time to reign, we must understand God's plan and purpose in the cross, and His complete protection of His Son prior to the cross. And in a sense during the cross, because victory was accomplished, nothing touched Him apart from the Father's will. An 'hour's brief but recorded time before the complete victory of the cross was accomplished over darkness, deeds of darkness, the torture of unforgiveness.

The hell of darkness as a choice to be outside Christ

There is darkness when God removes His presence and power as in a time of judgement. It can be God's hand that brings disaster. In response to our own wickedness, He banishes us. It is a very harsh word, it means total separation. And it is into darkness that He banishes us. We need to understand the need for repentance, to confess our sins to one another and to be forgiven. We can also choose this total separation, by being outside Christ, rejecting His love and forgiveness. If a man or woman chooses to reject Jesus forever it is total separation, eternally banished from His presence, power, protection and love. All that we fear about darkness stays real because we refuse to acknowledge Christ His power presence and protection. We *"will be thrown outside into the darkness where there will be weeping and gnashing of teeth." (Matthew 22:13).* There is a point to darkness, in this life but victory over the evil of darkness has to be a real choice. That choice is only possible as we confess, repent of our sin and accept Jesus. We can have the same fears in and outside Christ. Inside Christ we are to choose the truth of God's word. Outside Christ we are to choose to be saved, by that same word. *(Romans 10:9-10,13; John 3:16-18).*

Chapter 3

The necessity of the protective cover of darkness

D ARKNESS is our hiding place. We often want to hide, because of hurt, pain even shame, or from danger. Darkness is as light to the Lord. We cannot hide from the Lord, but He can give us a hiding place. A place of rest secure from being found. He can hide even heal because of the solace of privacy. *"Surely the darkness will hide me and the light become night around me."*(Psalm 139:11). We need a place of privacy, a place of protection, a place of security from too glaring a light. *"You are my hiding – place; you will protect me from trouble and surround me with songs of deliverance" (Psalm 32:7).* We can go to the Lord as our hiding place, not to hide from the Lord but from other men. Because it is *"when the wicked rise to power, men go into hiding." (Proverbs 28:12, 28).* To hide ourselves is different from concealing our sin. We often need a safe place. Scripture implies that we do not thrive, under these circumstances, but are still kept safe until the righteous rise to power. Moses was hidden in those famous reeds. David went into hiding when Saul tried to take His life having been told *"Be on your guard tomorrow morning go into hiding and stay there." (1 Samuel 19:2).* Light can appear too cruel and damaging if forced on us. God also gives place for that. *(Acts 9:1-9).* To be exposed for wrong doing is in my opinion God's last resort if we do not repent privately. Even the fact we are hurt, cannot be known to ourselves, until the light reveals this to us. This can be through knowing another person who is more whole or healed than us. Or through reading, psychology, even child psychology. God is our hiding place, a place of protection and refuge. There are times in our lives when we just choose to hide. Darkness especially physical is not necessarily a bad state, but a canopy to hide from our enemies, from people who hurt us from real danger. We are hidden because we fear being hurt, or our pain and wounding too deep for us to seek anything, but privacy. Sometimes we hide because we have wronged another. It is our God who can choose to hide us in that terrible state and lead us through to a place of repentance and righteousness. We cannot ever hide from God but He can hide us safely. God's growth occurs in darkness, as darkness can hide us like a protective canopy as we form develop and grow. This is a spiritual truth which also has a parallel in the physical world. Spiritual realities are often reflected in the physical world

> A child in the mother's womb, pitch black darkness.
> A seed underground, eventually totally dependant on light to live.
> A photograph has its image on a dark film to become a feature of the light.

The cover of darkness can also be a form of protection

Light can be like darkness, too bright for us to see. It is blinding. That was Saul's state in disobedience. We can fear God, and be in obedience, and still have a night. We are to trust God.

The light can sometimes be too painful for us not to be hidden. We are unable to hide from God, from His loving kindness and healing. He is with us. *(Psalm 139:6-10)*. But we can hide from prying eyes from the taunts of wicked men. The Lord himself makes darkness His canopy. *(Isaiah 45:15;2 Samuel 22:12)*. He also dwells in a dark cloud. There is sometimes a desire to be in physical darkness in times of suffering. This is different from spiritual darkness and deeds of darkness, there is no evil or evil intent. There is little reference in God's word of the cover of the physical night being for evil, and times of light used for hiding. *"In the dark, men break into houses, but by day they shut themselves;" (Job 24: 16).* Hiding is referred to in a Godly sense of solace and protection.

There is often working *"in the dark"*, any craftsman will work in privacy even secrecy. Sometimes entirely alone, at other time a few are allowed to enter. So with our God: *"He who began a good work in you will carry it on to completion." (Philippians 1:6).* God works in secret, in secret places in our inner most being, in darkness. He will, as with a potter pleased with His work, exhibit and bring into the light, the methods used, and the skill of His workmanship. This happens sometimes never; His craftsmanship hidden. So with us God holds us up like stars in the universe. We are seen as letters written on another's heart.

People write letters privately to be seen by another, but not to be a public item. There is a difference between walking in the light, and being a public person

Darkness

i) It protects from harm. God can work in the darkness because darkness is as light to Him. God's enemies and our enemies, which are hopefully the same, want to destroy us, to destroy God's good work which He has started in us. The dark prevents an enemy seeing God's way, this makes it difficult for them to harm. Enemies do not know what good is happening until it is seen, they do not know God. As soon as the light shines on God's good work, they will try attack and undermine that work. What God has started He will bring to completion. *(Philippians 1:6)*. This applies to God's spiritual and concrete work. Scans shining light on a baby forming are neither allowed numerically, nor past a certain date because it is too intrusive. They are formed secretly. An enemy will want to destroy that hidden process.

ii) It protects from wrong exposure as with light on a film. Processing a film is skilled, as is the amount of light used in the 'dark developing room'.

iii) Darkness hides us from our enemies. An enemy's attack causes detrimental changes. It is God's hand and clinging to His word, with understanding that enables us to go through the darkest night. *"Though I sit in darkness the Lord will be my light" (Micah 7:8)*. There is an understanding in scripture that although we can be in darkness God remains our light.

There are some things that are best not hidden

and that is LOVE. We are not to hide or withhold our love. But we are to hide ourselves from harm and danger spiritual and physical.

<u>Our choice can be to hide from:</u>

a) God, like Adam and eve when they sinned; *(Genesis 3:8,10)* and Jonah from the responsibility to preach, but this is not possible. He is omnipresent. If we make our bed in the depths He is still there. *(Psalm139:8).*

b) From each other *(Genesis3:7)*

c) From the world, its evil and its pace. *"When the wicked rise to power, men go into hiding." (Proverbs 28:12) "Hide me in the shadow of your wings from the wicked who assail me." (Psalm 17: 8)* The psalmist asked to be hidden from the conspiracy of the wicked. We are to hide from the evil plots of men.

d) From ourselves. We have the inability to face the truth about who we are, either our ability, or our deficiencies. Our goodness, or our wickedness. We want to hide, and to cover ourselves.

e) From our faults *"Who can discern his errors?*

Forgive my hidden faults."(Psalm 19:12). We also hide our wrong doing, because of shame, pain, and an inability to accept the reality about ourselves. It is seen not as our fault.

f) From danger. God Himself is our hiding place. *"You are my hiding – place; you will protect me from trouble and surround me with songs of deliverance" (Psalm 32:7).* God can also instruct us specifically to a place of safety. *"Go to the hills so that the pursuers will not find you. Hide yourselves there three days until they return, and then go on your way." (Joshua 2:16; 1 Samuel 19:2).*

g) For protection. We can hide, precious things are hidden. Treasures of wisdom, and knowledge are hidden in Christ. *"The mystery of God, namely, Christ in whom are hidden all the treasures of wisdom and knowledge." (Colossians 2:2-3).* Our lives are now hidden with Christ in God. *(Colossians 3:3).* We are hidden.

h) From the intrigues of men, as a choice of privacy. We hide because we do not choose for there to be an invasion of our privacy. *"In the shelter of your presence you hide them from the intrigues of men; in your dwelling you keep them safe from accusing tongues." (Psalm 31:20).*

Hidden from gossip and malicious talk.

i) We can also use darkness to hide our best, for fear of being seen to be gifted, talented or more gifted and talented than others. In case we are seen to be different, or beautiful in some way. Because of fear of ridicule or because if our best is seen and rejected, there is pain. This hiding can be due to lack of self acceptance, or jealousy of others. People's best work is usually done in secret, hidden from most. And when it is their choice to work in physical darkness, as well as private. The work as a public item can be difficult to find. Some people do their best work in secrecy in a hidden place sometimes in darkness, with little light. But it is also true that what is done in secret, will be known . Nothing is hidden from God. He is just. *(Psalm 44:21; Matthew 6:4; 1 Corinthians 14:25).*

Hiding is referred to in a Godly sense. A place of solace and protection. God expects us not to hide from Him, and that in reality it is not possible to hide from our creator God, but with Him and that He remains our refuge. He can find for us a 'hiding place', a place of privacy and protection. A place of healing and repentance without the glare of life's camera on us. As in Shakespeare *'All the world's a stage'*, but sometimes our choice is to hide from the world, and that stage.

Chapter 4

God's presence and help in the dark

GOD is in, and can be found in the darkness, an ever-present help in trouble. Darkness is as light to Him. He can lead and guide us through to a place of understanding of our safety, with an assurance of salvation and forgiveness, our righteousness in Him. He can bring us through to a place of being more spiritually mature, with spiritual revelation, and understanding. Darkness is caused spiritually when we doubt God's word, or we do not know the truth of that word. We have not understood that not to obey God will cause spiritual darkness, whether this is because of fear, rebellion or unbelief. We loose our way, getting lost we loose our faith, as well as an ability to accept the truth of God's word. In the darkest situations the light dawns as we believe in God.

God's guidance in the darkness

We function more naturally in the light, as opposed to darkness. It is a more natural state. If there is a power cut we will naturally reach for a candle, to light, or a torch, or find a place, with light! We use head-lamps street lamps reflectors. It is a safer, more navigatable way. All an indication of the necessity of light spiritually, to find the right path, to grow and develop. So in our lives we need the life of Christ, and His light, to lead the way. The life of Christ was the light. The light of Christ in others also helps.

It is very important the way in which we live when we have the light. It is still the light and not the darkness we are to trust. Most activities that we do are in the day. And if done by night we use artificial light, because we need to be able, to see. *"Put your trust in the light while you have it, so you may become sons of light." (John12:35-36).* In a spiritual way, we also need as much spiritual light as possible. Even when we have had the light and known the way, when darkness comes even in a familiar place, there is unknown. Even the most familiar path in total darkness cannot be walked safely, to continue we need the light. The light is God's word, Jesus is the word made flesh.

God is a *"guide for the blind, a light for those who are in the dark." (Romans 2:19).* He is with us lighting the way, *"a light shining in a dark place, until the day dawns and the morning star rises in your hearts." (2 Peter 1:19).* God can guide us by His light in darkness, darkness is as light to Him. He promises to guide us. We have the light of God's word, as we walk by faith, which is a lamp for our path. He guides us through to a place of light in a spiritual sense. A place of understanding. God knows the way we take and can guide us through the darkest night. The terror of the night, through the unknown of the spiritual night. It will have been our choice, on accepting Jesus as our Lord and saviour, having believed on His name, to walk in the light of Christ.

We are to walk while we have the light, when night comes we are to be familiar with God's path, not to fear Him or His way. Because when darkness comes we cease to walk. As a Christian we should never make the choice to walk in darkness because we have the light of Christ, God's word. It is a lamp for our feet. We are to hold one another spiritually in our dark night. We are not always to be in darkness, because of our inability to let the word of Christ in, we are to accept the truth of God's word. It may be because we have not hidden God's word in our hearts or because we are outside the saving knowledge and light of Christ. Darkness is not a normal state within the Kingdom of God. We have our nights of trial and temptation. It is often the unknown and the inability to accept God knows the way that causes us to fear darkness, and not to welcome its solace, peace, and privacy.

Those outside Christ are in darkness and for them to walk through to a place of victory they have to learn of Jesus, to be given those treasures they need to come to a saving knowledge of Jesus. We can be saved; we are to call upon the name of Jesus. *"Brothers, my hearts desire and prayer to God is that.....you might be saved" (Romans 10: 1). "That if you confess with your mouth, "Jesus is Lord" and believe in your heart God raised Him from the dead, and you will be saved." (Romans 10: 9).* Some might say: 'How do I believe in my heart.' Pray God gives you the ability and grace to believe in your heart, that God raised Jesus from the dead, because even faith is a gift from God. It is *"with your heart that you believe and are justified, and with your mouth that you confess and are saved. " (Romans 10:10).*

Outside Christ there are 'sign-posts' to lead us to Christ, the Godly lives of other, God's hand at work in events and circumstances and His word. Because darkness, without God's presence, is a place of torture and confusion formless and empty. We must be inside Christ saved.

God is light and in Him there is no darkness. We having chosen to follow Jesus have chosen to walk in and be the light. But we live in relationship with people, even the most isolated of us. It is in that place of relationship or fall out of relationship that we can find ourselves in a 'night of darkness' through no fault or choice of our own. It can be the other person or group of people, who choose to put us in darkness by lying to us, deceiving us or withholding information. Jesus shares with us His deepest secrets of loving wisdom. This can happen in relationship with others outside Christ, in the domain of darkness, and inside Christ in the kingdom of light.

Relationship is different from fellowship, in that we are only able to be in fellowship if we are in the light and that is only possible inside Christ. We are instructed not to associate with the violent, nor to eat with the sexually immoral *(1 Corinthians 5:9, 11)*. They are people who walk in darkness choosing the deeds of darkness. We can be deceived unless the light of Christ shines in such a way to expose them, or we have a word of knowledge or insight we associate with them and eat with them. *(Matthew 13:24-30)*. We are to pray that we are not dragged away with evil and wicked men, that we have enough discernment to distinguish, truth and righteousness, from error. A man or woman in darkness, from one in the light. We can be deceived with lies, and even lured by darkness, but we are to learn God's lessons in darkness and gain spiritual wisdom and insight. There will be a separation of the righteous from the wicked. *(Matthew 13:49)*. God will *"weed out everything that causes us to sin and all who do evil." (Matthew 13:40-42).*

On having confessed our sin and repented of that sin, and having accepted the greatest treasure, Jesus, in our hearts and lives so we can go into dark places with His presence, protection understanding His ways and saving grace. We are then inside Christ with God's people. We have God's word as a lamp to guide us as we walk by faith. People outside Christ have the same word to guide them; to the love, mercy, and forgiveness of Jesus, and to, the cross of Christ. But even when we have chosen to walk in the light of Christ to the best of our ability, knowledge, and understanding we end up in a place of darkness.

We are in darkness because:

a) Because of our sinful nature: *"For I have the desire to do what is good but I can not carry it out" (Romans 7:18). "For what I want to do I do not do, but what I hate to do." (Romans 7:15).*

b) Other people's choice. They choose to sin against us, connect us to their sin and to lie about us. They slander, and too few people know the truth. The truth may only be known to us. It is an evil, and destructive choice for a person to make. Possibly a fearful one, so another person is in the *'same boat'*. We are not to choose deeds of darkness, in a night of trial. Sin against us can hurt, overwhelm, and mar us enough; to choose deeds of darkness, as if on the world's side. We are to pray our faith will not fail. Our desire is to be, to take refuge in God, clinging and cleaving closer to Him and His word. We are to take refuge in physically safe place. It is also our own deception, and our acceptance knowingly of another's deception and sin including against us that will cause us, this same choice.

c) Our lack of discernment. We choose unwittingly friends who have chosen deeds of darkness, or we become unequally yoked to an unbeliever a person outside Christ. They are in darkness, and are choosing to walk in darkness not known to us.

A couple can be put in darkness through no fault of their own having been deceived and lied to, and about. That relationship remains a night unless both a husband and wife choose to walk in the light of the gospel of Christ together. There is still light as we rely on God's presence. God can give wisdom and knowledge about reality. This is important as other's deception can affect our mental health. God reveals the truth to us about people, about events and circumstances by

His Holy Spirit. We are anointed by His Holy Spirit. *"Satan himself masquerades as an angel of light." (2 Corinthians 11:14).* People can masquerade as servants of righteousness.We have the Spirit of Christ within us, born again of the Holy Spirit. He will give us wisdom as to the reality of people's hearts.

Satan fell like lightening. But people who masquerade as *'angels of light'* have made dark spiritual choices, to do evil with evil intent, choosing wicked deeds of darkness but appear as light. We are not to be like them but to fear God and to shun evil. *"For our struggle is not against flesh and blood, but against the rulers against the authorities against the powers of this dark world and against the spiritual forces of evil." (Ephesians 6:12).*

d) Our fault. We choose to sin, choose to lie about ourselves, or another person. It is because of our disobedience that we can be in darkness. *"At midday you will grope around like a blind man in the dark." (Deuteronomy 28:29).* He can hide His face from us because of sin; we are to again find His glory. We are to know that there is hope even when He has put us in the darkest pit. He may choose to put us in darkness. *"You have put me in the lowest pit, in the darkest depths."(Psalm 88:6).*

e) We loose our way spiritually. He may put us in

darkness until we cope.

f) Like Jesus we have the darkest night of the cross put on our lives through no fault of of our own. If we enter a dark night because we have accepted another's sin and deception, and sinned ourselves. We will at some point have to choose to repent of the choice to err. This means we will still go into a cross like trial as our sinful nature is crucified, as we allow God's word to guide us again. We can learn to walk spiritually through to a place of light. God's word is light to us, in the darkest place and understood leads us through to a place of victory. And if the night that surrounds us is too difficult the love of Christ carries us through. Darkness should be temporary as night is to day, so will our darkness not remain. No-one, in Christ who believes in Jesus should stay in darkness. *(John 12:46)*. The knowledge that the night ends and treasures are formed in and given to us in that night gives hope, reason and purpose. As we go through the night coming forth as gold this understanding sustains, enabling us to cope. The night can seem meaningless, the truth makes that night meaningful as we wait for God's resurrection power and perspective.

Chapter 5

Treasures of Darkness

THERE are times of refining, when God allows us to go through suffering to bring about His plan and purpose. We are to believe it is His hand of grace, and mercy that are at work, working all things together for our good. We are not to harden our hearts when on the receiving end of cruelty, either cruel events or cruel people. As we learn obedience through suffering, we will learn His will, and His way. God will not tempt us beyond that which we are able to bear. We learn to walk spiritually through to a place of light. God's word is light to us in the darkest place, understood leads us through to a place of victory and strength. It can be because of our disobedience that we are in darkness. Our obedience leads to victory. We can experience darkness because of God's will, His set purpose and foreknowledge. There is purpose in our trial. It is God's plan we are given those treasures and have those secrets shared with us. Always understand there is purpose and victory in God's economy. He is always working to create, for our good. People without God's grace cannot make their nights days, nor turn their formless empty, darkness into treasure. It is important that we understand that we need God, His grace and anointing. It is God's will and working in us that creates treasure. They can be seen in our lives, and in the making of our character.

God turns darkness into light

He changes wounds, and scars by His grace into healing, a triumph of His grace. Forgiven sin and its darkness into a victory over satan. Jesus is light, and His word spoken into our darkness, heals and brings understanding. Our lives can be transformed, as we are changed from one degree of glory to another. As we become more light, accepting God's word so we give more light to others. There is more life in us. Our darkness of thought, action, and state, is due to our own sin and the sin of others against us. Another's sin and sometimes a wilful attempt to put us into a trial of darkness, is a cross.

Treasures of creation were made from what was formless, dark and empty. Treasures are given to us, and our character formed in sometimes the deepest darkness. As we learn to appropriate:

i) God's word, the entrance of that word gives light.

ii) And to confess our sin, as well as our state of

darkness, and confusion, and feelings of the unknown.

iii) And let Christ in. There are treasures of wisdom and understanding as we simply **wait for a 'night' to end.**

God will give us treasures of darkness. Children love treasures, and we are children of God. *(1 John 3:1; John 1:12).* Children are treasures, gifts from God.

Treasures of understanding God's will, God's way and His word.

Treasures of being changed into His likeness becoming more Christ-like. As we are changed from one degree of glory to another.

Treasures of being central to His will and closer to His heart.

Treasures wrought out in our lives as God's plan is fulfilled in our lives, as we learn to rely on our God, and to walk by faith. God is unchanging. He is the same yesterday, today and forever.

Treasures of wisdom, knowledge and understanding that are hid in Christ. *"In bringing many sons to glory, it was fitting that God, for whom and through whom everything exists, should make the author of their salvation perfect through suffering." (Hebrews 2:10).* There are riches stored in secret places. Diamonds, jewels and treasures. They are made in the deepest, darkest places of the earth, under the highest pressures and heat. But beautiful they are and beautiful they stay. That purifying work cannot be reversed. Once a diamond always a diamond. God will not waste one tear, heartache, nor the suffering of one fear. He will bring salvation to us, His saving grace. He will have planted desires in our hearts, and will bring His plan and purpose to fulfilment.

The fear and the unbelief that God is good that can cause us to give up, and to fall into sin choosing the deeds of darkness instead of understanding our night of trial. As well as the unbelief that all things are possible with God, and that all things work together for our good. We need reward. God rewards those who earnestly seek Him. God comes to us in the darkness, as other people will to shine His light, the light of Christ into our hearts to encourage us. But whether due to discouragement we choose to sin or because our hearts become hardened because of unbelief. We give up. It is the cross and the resulting grace that enables those treasures to be formed and given. Without the cross and the victory of the cross there is still just the darkness, formless, empty, frightening, with the negative realities and implications of that darkness as evil. It is God's ability to overcome the negative of darkness, and our understanding of God's presence and protection in darkness that gives victory. Our judgement and sin was atoned for by Jesus on the cross. Another person however much we choose to maim, hurt, abuse and to use them as scapegoats cannot pay the price they cannot forgive our sin, nor bring God's plan and purpose to fulfilment. They cannot save us eternally. Jesus crucifixion was once and for all a finished work to be made real in our lives as we accept Him. We are to confess Jesus is Lord, and believe in our hearts, God raised Him from the dead to be saved, and enter into Gods unique plan for our lives. We are to confess our sins to one another. It is the accomplished finished work of the cross that secures our eternal salvation, from death, hell and destruction. This finished work cannot be accomplished in any other way. People are not to be used as scapegoats as sacrificial lambs. We are not to hurt or harm for our gain. As I understand there are sacrificial rituals of a barbaric kind in devil worship, they are deeds of darkness. These will not bring forgiveness, the gospel of Christ will. We are not to crucify Him again in another human being. Seemingly perfect people, anointed to forgive, as God's people, are not sinless and perfect. Because we all have fallen short of God's glory and sinned. Along with those they choose to forgive they too go to throne of grace for forgiveness. Jesus was perfect in obedience and sinless, able to forgive.

We are not to fear darkness including in a spiritual sense. We live in a world of darkness, full of deeds of darkness, in which we are the light. *(Colossians 1:13)*. The deeds of darkness are often carried out directly against us. We are in Christ and have been rescued from the domain of darkness, and deeds of darkness. There is a spiritual battle in the darkness connected to unbelief. We do not believe in the truth of God's word. We can fear eternal separation from God, and being assigned with evil. We are to conquer the sin of fear and unbelief by accepting the truth of God's word. We fear God's judgement as a result of sin. It is a real battle to defeat the lies of satan.

Fear of being outside Christ, and eternally condemned are for the unsaved to accept Jesus and for us to cleave to Him and the truth of His saving grace.

God is able, because of the finished work of the cross, to reverse our disasters, and bring us through to a place of loving victory. It is God's redemptive work. As we choose to walk in obedience, so God prospers us. It is love that triumphs over evil, the devil, and the hate of others, that prevents God's plan and purpose.

We need much encouragement in the darkest times. We are also to understand not to give up hope, but to give thanks, because in His Son we are still qualified to share in His inheritance *"to the praise of His glory." (Ephesians 1:13-14; Colossians 1:12).* As a believer in the Lordship of Jesus Christ, we do not in reality, in our darkest times become separated, from the grace and the kingdom of God. No-one can snatch us from His hand. *"Having believed, you were marked in Him with a seal, the promised Holy Spirit who is a deposit guaranteeing our inheritance until the redemption of those who are God's possession." (Ephesians 1:13; 2 Corinthians 1: 22, 5:5).* But if we do not accept God's forgiveness, and respond to His word in obedience, we put ourselves in a place of judgement until we reach a position of faith. In accepting the truth of God's word, it is both passive relating to our position, and active in obeying His instructions and commands. We are to cling to God's word in the darkest times of the unknowing so that we might become, and understand those treasures; choosing God's will and way. We are not to choose times of trial, and darkness, but of blessing. The merit of darkness is to hide in times of pain and from our enemies. We are not to shrink back and choose to walk in deeds of darkness, over seeking God's light and understanding. We are not to choose sickness, sin and deeds of darkness. It is the way in which we respond to God's dark night that is of imperative importance.

"God will weed out of His Kingdom everything that

causes us to sin and do evil" (Matthew 13:41). His will is to refine and to purify us. We are not to fear the darkness of the cross. God will never leave nor forsake us, even in our darkest night.

We need to rely on God, His faithfulness, His word and in prayer, until we have faith and peace. *(Philippians 4:6-7; Matthew 7:7).* People become lost in the dark, physically lost, and lost as a person. They become lost through disobedience, sin and lack of understanding. It is our lack of understanding that enables the devil to deceive. It is as we overcome fear, and faith is formed, and understood that a treasure is given. As we understand how to love as opposed to hate. As well as trusting Him, His love power and invincibility. **Darkness can happen because of the element of impossibility, the task appears too overwhelming and too large.**

Why have I chosen "Treasures of Darkness" because people hide themselves in the dark. They are treasures to God, precious and honoured in His sight. We need to understand them, find them, their gifts and talents. We need to understand God's refining in the dark.

We often miss the best in another, because we do not wait to see the fulfilment of God's work in their lives. They are in a time of trial, and darkness. We are to wait for the jewel, in them, to be seen as God has worked His will, way and character into their person. We will just have encountered their dark night. There is always, in the kingdom of God, a point to suffering. And to darkness an end. There is no darkness in heaven.

"There will be no more night. They will not need the light of a lamp or the light of the sun, for the Lord God will give them light." (Revelations 22:5).

The best is hidden because our wisdom is not deep enough; our spiritual eyes not discerning enough, our insight not sharp enough. It is with deep intimacy with God that we learn His ways.

There is the brilliance of invention not seen, known, or understood, unless pointed out and explained. We need to look for hidden treasures in each other. Our assets and abilities, gifts talents as well as our hidden beauty. God has formed our inner most being. As well as the hidden treasures of other people's work, including invention. We purchased a children's game, the skill of assembly was to be marvelled at, also giving insight into the working of a man's intelligence and reasoning to accomplish that task. Their ability was for all to see. There is instruction for us to do things in secret. Our giving is not to be publicly done, nor on display.

The fact remains we live in a dark world, satan's domain of darkness into which we pray *"your kingdom come, your will be done on earth as it is in heaven." (Matthew 6:10).* His kingdom is a kingdom of light. We are in this dark world as light to the truth, reality and hope of Jesus Christ, our greatest treasure. We are guiding posts to Jesus, who is the way the truth and the life. The fact remains that we also have dark nights of suffering spiritually and physically. Nights of loss, sorrow, pain and of temptation. We can not live as if night is not a reality for some, and the darkness of night a choice for others.

As believers, we live in the kingdom of light, that is believers in the deity of Christ, *(John1: 34;5:18).* He is God and the Son of God, in the crucifixion *(Galatians 5:24; John 19:23).* and the resurrection, and the virgin birth *(Luke 23:44-46;Matthew 27:53).* The crucifixion His darkest night and ours. *"I have been crucified with Christ and I no longer live, but Christ lives in me…The life I live … I live by faith." (Galatians 2:20).* Jesus is our atoning sacrifice. He is able to forgive our sins. When light dawns in our hearts, there is an understanding God, because of the price paid by Jesus on the cross, wipes our slate clean. Sin that separated us from God and put us in eternal hell is forgiven. This understanding is a treasure and a miracle. Jesus's forgiveness secured on the cross enables us to be seated in heavenly places in Christ Jesus; and puts us into the kingdom of light in the Son whom He loves. On choosing to become a child of God that reality becomes known to us.

One assumes if you are spiritually blind, as when physically blind you cannot see the brilliance of God's work within a person nor the way. The truth of God's word and the reality of that word at work within. We cannot follow the way, the truth and the life, Jesus. It is our and others sin, sickness and evil that cut us off from the light, and presence of God. There is a presence of darkness in our person, we are not seen as we really are in Christ. Our treasures cannot be seen.

It would have not been known or understood, to most that Jesus on that cross was the greatest victor, of all. Victor over death, sin, sickness, evil, satan's plan, over hatred, jealousy, over separation from His Father in Heaven, and from His creation, including man. It was just three days further on from that crucifixion, His darkest night that His total victory was seen, and secured. His eternal work accomplished. And begun on earth in the hearts and lives of men reversing the effects of the devil, that was caused in the Garden of Eden; total separation from God and each other. On the cross Jesus secured our forgiveness, and our place in the heavenlies in Christ Jesus. We are in the light, and in the Kingdom of the Son whom He loves, even in our darkest night. The outworking of the cross, its salvation and saving grace is secured eternally because it is a finished work, but we see its outworking in the present in our lives. That is as:

a) A Supernatural happening as we believe in Jesus calling upon His name *(Romans 10: 13)*. In an instant we are transferred from the kingdom of darkness into the kingdom of light.

b) A Daily choice: It is also due to our daily choice to be in the light, to continue to let the truth of God's word into our hearts and minds daily. It is God's word that is light. As sign posts to guide the way, as we follow their instructions daily so God directs our path. It is our choice to walk in truth and honesty. There needs to be only a little light to walk safely especially if the path is known to us. For us, in the light of Christ, in obedience to His word there should be a blaze of light. There is a choice of good deeds over deeds of darkness.

It is my prayer even in our darkest night that we do not rebel against God's will and way and choose deeds of darkness *(Romans 13:12)*, but choose to walk more closely into the love and light of the gospel of Christ choosing God's will. That we continue to choose to be rich in good deeds. *(1 Timothy 6:18; Ephesians 5:11)*. Our choice even in the darkest night is to do good. *(1 Peter 2: 20)*. Remembering darkness is as light to Him. We are to choose to rely on our God, understand His will, way, and teaching, in the refiner's fire. That we understand that the most beautiful stones are made in places of darkness. And that is where God's treasure and secrets are kept. But that it is our choice to shine the most brilliantly, as we stay faithful to the gospel of Christ, as we traverse our night to find day. For the fruit of the light consists in all goodness, our good deeds, spring from our faith. We are not to use our freedom for license, nor sin more than God's grace is able to abound. We are not to change the grace of God into license. *(Jude 1:4)*. Our love must be sincere, hate what is evil cling to what is good. We are to continue to do good. *(1 Peter 4:19)*. Even if we choose the fruitless deeds of darkness, we will in time suffer as much if not more than if we had endured the night, of the cross. No-one can snatch us from God's hand.

If we have walked well while we have had the light of Christ, and have understood, and been obedient to His word so we will be carried through the darkest path secure in the knowledge of God's love. Even darkness is as light to the Lord so we are not to fear His hand, which is also in the darkness. We are to learn to recognize His presence. We must understand darkness is as light to Him, and He knows the way. And that we are in Him, born again by the Holy Spirit. We have the deposit of God's Holy Spirit guaranteeing what is to come. We are not to fear His refining hand, we are to be secure in the knowledge of His love, He will not leave nor forsake us.

Physical darkness is not inheritantly bad or evil but it can be frightening because it brings into our lives the element of the unknown. In physical darkness we use lights to navigate, so in spiritual darkness we are to use God's word to navigate through a difficult time. BLESSED is the man who perseveres under trial because....He will receive the crown of life. Where the Spirit of the Lord is there is freedom, but we are to be careful how we use our freedom. We are not to cover up evil.

We are given those treasures of darkness because in His giving, we will know He is Lord. It is God's entire powerful plan, not man's, not satan's, but His plan, the Lords' plan and purpose that prevails. *"I know you can do all things no plan of yours can be thwarted." (Job 42:2).* Jesus is Lord, and those treasures can be ours in Christ.

Epilogue

Just as the night ends and becomes day so our night ends. *(Revelations 21:25; 22:5)*

"'This is what the Lord says to his anointed, to Cyrus, whose right hand I take hold of to subdue nations before him and to strip kings of their armour, to open doors before him so that gates will not be shut: I will go before you and will level the mountains.' I will break down gates of bronze and cut through bars of iron. I will give you the treasures of darkness, riches stored in secret places so that you may know that I am the Lord the God of Israel who summons you by name..I am the Lord there is no other. I form the light and create the darkness." (Isaiah 45:1-3; 7).